Praise for Sam Cheuk

"This playful, deeply philosophical collection plays good cop and bad cop with the reader… *Love Figures* shines light in our eyes, interrogates us endlessly and begs us to stare at ourselves in the mirror with the full knowledge that there are others staring back at us, just on the other side of our reflection."

— Catriona Wright, *Maple Tree Literary Supplement*

"I stopped to look at Sam Cheuk's *Deus et Machina* at a small press show in London because it's a beautiful… I bought it though, because the strength of its voice caught at me even as I was just flipping through it. Lines like, "The mouth is a wound; where can pain expire if it's stitched up?" wouldn't let me put it back on the table without giving it a proper read. I laid down my money and read it twice before the show was over, twice more the next day. "

— Jeremy Luke Hill, *The Town Crier*

Postscripts from a City Burning

Postscripts from a City Burning

Sam Cheuk

Palimpsest Press
1171 Eastlawn Ave.
Windsor, Ontario, N8S 3J1
www.palimpsestpress.ca

Printed and bound in Canada
Cover design and book typography by Ellie Hastings
Edited by Jim Johnstone
Cover photo by Chris Gaul

Palimpsest Press would like to thank the Canada Council for the Arts
and the Ontario Arts Council for their support of our publishing
program. We also acknowledge the assistance of the Government of
Ontario through the Ontario Book Publishing Tax Credit.

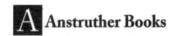

LIBRARY AND ARCHIVES CANADA CATALOGUING IN PUBLICATION

TITLE: Postscripts of a city burning / Sam Cheuk.
NAMES: Cheuk, Sam, 1980- author.
DESCRIPTION: Poems.
IDENTIFIERS: Canadiana (print) 20210266511
             Canadiana (ebook) 20210266562

ISBN 9781989287811 (SOFTCOVER)
ISBN 9781989287828 (EPUB)
ISBN 9781989287880 (PDF)

CLASSIFICATION: LCC PS8605.H4747 P67 2021 | DDC C811/.6—DC23

Table of Contents

For Elaine

"'Giving shape to time is especially important now, when the future is so shapeless.' What of time that feels like it's running out?"

— Varsha Gandikota-Nellutla, quoting Heidi Pitlor

CHARACTERS

STUDENTS/PROTESTERS   Black-clad, gas
                       mask, yellow hard
                       hat. Leaderless.

JIMMY SHAM (岑子杰)   Leader of Civil
                       Human Rights Front
                       (CHRF): "This election
                       is special because it
                       is a formal confrontation
                       between pro-establishment
                       and pro-democracy
                       parties after months
                       of unrest caused by
                       the misstep of
                       government."

CHRIS TANG (鄧炳強)   New Hong Kong Police
                       Chief: "Believing
                       such fake news would
                       lead to a low credibility
                       of the force, but surely
                       we will also review
                       whether we should be
                       more transparent."

CARRIE LAM (林鄭月娥)   Chief Executive of
                       Hong Kong: "If I have
                       a choice, the first thing
                       is to quit, having made
                       a deep apology, then
                       step down."

CITIZEN

SETTING

An ex-British colony and global financial hub, nexus through which western investments flow into China, and vice versa. Deemed a Special Administrative Region of China for that reason; "One Country, Two Systems" is enacted here, allowing the harbour city to keep "Common Law," the inherited British governance and legal framework, as long as it doesn't supersede "Basic Law," the rule of law of China.

TIME

A fumbled attempt at passing an extradition amendment law that would establish an extradition accord between Hong Kong and China, ill-received by Hong Kong citizenry.

China and the USA are in the midst of a trade war. Prior to this, attempts were made by China to erode the British judicial and governmental framework.

Sorry I haven't written lately, winter is fast approaching, etc. Neither the emperor or the students have any clothes. Fortified behind their respective walls of legislature and campus, the police in between are prying at a resolution, trying to storm a burning bridge while students stand pat or slip into sewer grates. Beside it one of the city's arterial tunnels connects the island to the mainland, suspended, day 3.

Molotovs blossom everywhere. Overseas diners debate behind a glass pane, staff jamming wet towels under the front door, about the merit of a reporter who ran past, disappeared into smoke.

The PLA made a guest appearance yesterday, parading down a local street to clear it of its bricks.

I've been scribbling for poems, plucked off the streets last night a used gas canister I use as paper weight for luck, size of a cicada's shell. What's left inside don't smell so bad but I won't tempt the gods, ma.

10/29/19

A mood descends on a city,
call it fidelity maybe.

But it is not love, neither can its name
be mercy. Bodies are falling out
of high rises, ripened with meaning.
That deaths are supposed to turn
into something, they fall like fruit.

No, call it a chill.
Suspicious, we share plates, gossip.
News brings news and not much else,
scenery on fire. We are used to being
tired but not like this. Call it a way out,
a spiriting away.
                        There is necessarily
a villain in every story, but what if
it is the sun, if it brings the day,
and the day brings another day,
it keeps going, extends, chains.

Love, it is elsewhere—what is this terror,
not knowing what sheathes it into shape?

10/31/19

The eye sees what it knows:
rag, oil, bottle, enemy.
What refuses to make transparent:
skin, yearning, future tense.

How to mark and be marked
become our entirety then, a truce:
I don't know who I am, friend,
until I know who you are, foe.

Tables upon tables in this cafe
stretch across the city.
There will always be time
for fulsome chatter

but, if in a scorched moment,
in case I want to say hey, hello,
will you look up at me across
this divide, this ever widening space?

11/01/19

Someone finally died, love.
A stranger and I joked about it
under the guise of our mourning.

I've never wanted children, but I dreamt
of us having one. Hold this weight
for me, for a second. Somehow
let it become something beautiful,
or so goes the fantasy, a feint.

I simply want you to be here
without risking you being here. This can't
be our here. But I want to show you
the hometown I remember, where
I was a child once, these labyrinthine streets.

I don't know the story of the one who
died. I imagine he has stories
he wants of his own.
                              To give up a story,
I haven't the bravery.

It is beautiful here under the right weather—
a mistress moon behind fans of cloud,
tracers of taxi tail-lights beaconing the way
for the sprinting child, flapping in plastic sandals
towards a destination or an away,
with the certainty towards a where-to.

11/01/19 (2)

There is plenty of money to be made
in this chaos, he tells me. Words
I pretend to understand: implied
volatility, instrument, trading futures.

People arrive at these chances,
then leave. There is a scene
in a Ghibli film I grew up with,
the boy protagonist charges
against fleeing traffic into fire—
bombed homes for bread, pickled plums.

It's not fair to quote Arendt
if back home he has a wife, a daughter.
Love's surplus must subtract
from elsewhere, natural as an =.

To do right by those in my heart,
what violence will I be capable
of against you, your family,
an (x) scrubbed faceless?

11/02/19

Truth is fiction made real.
Between the caesura,
the next word made seen again;
there is the everyday, insisting
otherwise.
           I want to sit
with you, share a drink,
talk endlessly into the fiction
of what our lives could be.
I am here looking at you
looking at me.

The greatest trick ever conceived
by man is the messiness
of the in-between. I want to live
but how do we get there together?

Let's break things, break thru enough
things until the fictional world
unveils itself, and we can, thru
my image in your gaze see yours
in mine, be mirrors reproducing
each other endlessly.

11/03/19

It's impossible to take it all in
at once, this harbour.
That is the bridge where I protested
for the first time, when my 'rents took
me and thought it a good idea.
To the right, the convention centre
where protest happened tonight.
Further right, a high rise
a Japanese architect shaped
into the hilt of a sword, pointing
towards the colonial manor.
And behind that, I don't know if
you can see in the photo,
a mountain. Behind that, another
obscured from view, the story
of my genesis, a little foothill village
from where I used to hike up
to the peak, to be seen,
never then able to understand what
I was seeing.   This storied landscape,
these memories, others',
are what's at stake, even if
they can never be reclaimed.

While Nina Simone croons in my head,
"Stars, they come and go."
Water of the harbour undulates,
glimmer of the city's light tiding
before me.

11/04/19

They ran towards me
then passed. The generous I
wanted to ask *whom are you
running towards for?*
The harder part wanted to ask,
Stop. What I meant to say,
Don't run away from me.

We are always running towards
from something, we're all donning
masks we are ordained with,
is all. But even if ordained,
none of us would say no
to a home-cooked meal,
we're alike like that.

But you hold the gun. Non-lethal,
butt of your rifle a cotton candy pink,
as tho what you hold
isn't in the shape of a gun,
as tho the mask after work
can be left leaning against
your issued boots by the welcome mat.

Just as a beer bottle isn't the bottle
we, in a rosier time past,
would cincin to. Clink,
the crispness of the sound,
easy as a finger's twitch.

11/04/19 (2)

A citizen bit off another's ear.
Aunties, in front of the press,
become soothsayers
of the world. Halloween refuses
to end.
       To the seaside I keep
returning for my sanity,
for the sound of the sea
late at night, where no one
can see me. Worrying too
I might see the floating body
of a saint, who couldn't hold
it all in.
       Later on, in the foggy
morning I will prepare for work,
look into the mirror, comb my hair
and imagine each prick on my scalp
your fingers, adjust my tie, noosing me
together, so you have something
worth returning to.

11/05/19

My shirt falls onto the floor
in the shape of what it's supposed
to contain. Flabbergasted,
no one taught me how difficult
it was to pretend another's life
without striding in their shoes.

The steam of whatever I am
cooking smells about ready, think
it's convincing enough a lie for you
to believe. Needs cream,
maybe a little sugar, corn starch.
Gonna make a run downstairs,
the pot bubbling for an answer.

This home I have built awaits
another chair. So many new chairs
and cushions still covered in plastic
we wait to unwrap, wait for more
averting eyes around the table, waiting
for the next thing to happen,
so to plan, in case there are guests.

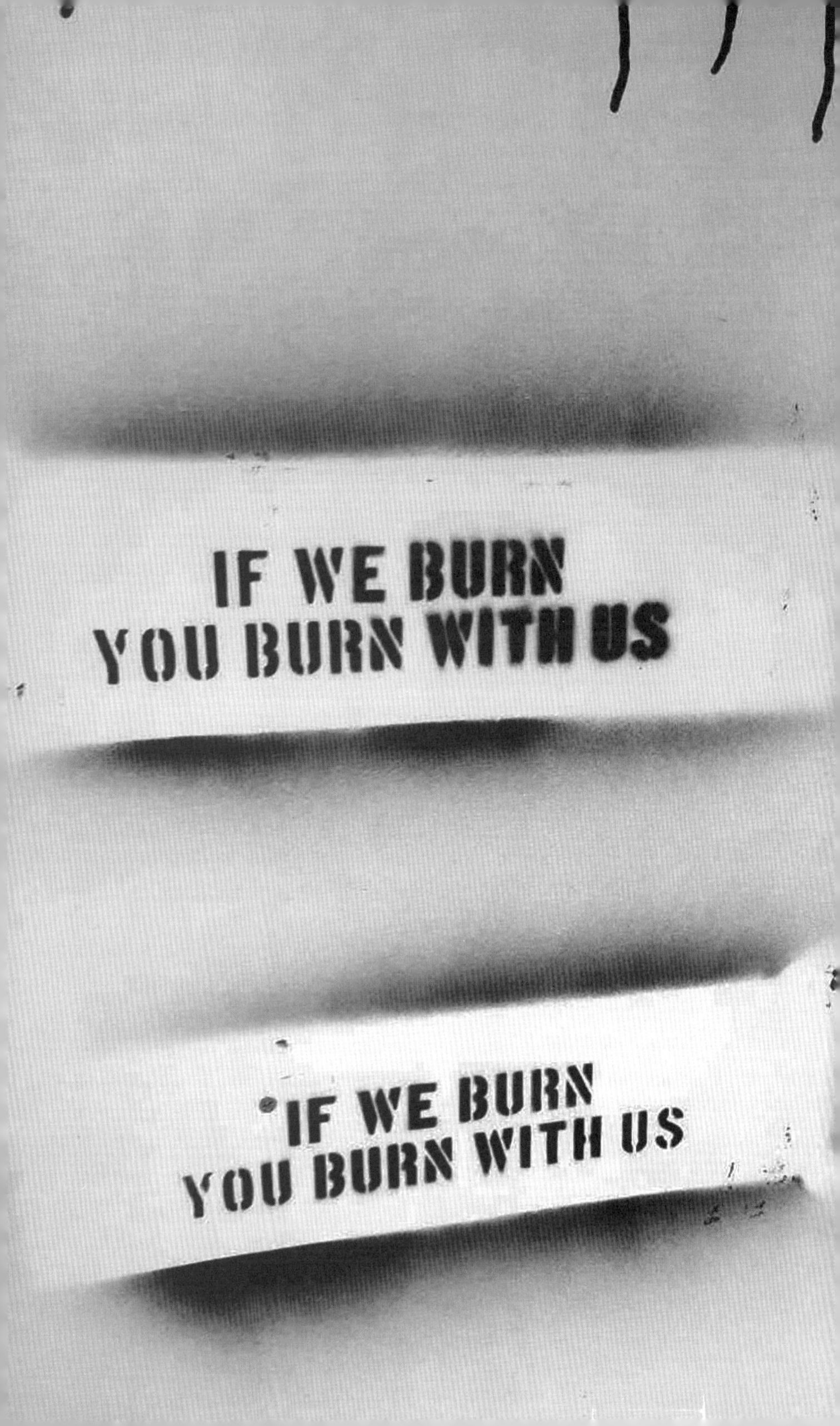
IF WE BURN
YOU BURN WITH US
IF WE BURN
YOU BURN WITH US

11/05/19 (2)

Don't betray me,
his brow suggests
behind a covering.

I offer him a beer
as reconciliation,
which he refuses
in the presence of
cops. It's not illegal
to drink publicly here,
I should mention.

I have sketched out
a park bench where
I envision us spacing
out, chugging beers
beside the soccer pitch,
trading daily nonsense
safe from the sirens.

Every line break
keeps threatening
towards articulation
when I want to write
effusively, leave room
for silliness, room
for nursery rhymes.
Where else can he
turn to? To us?

11/06/19

There's a new tradition
of politicians on the wrong
side stabbed without passion.
Security cameras keep looking
away, their irony unerring.

Then there's a student
on the ground, who knows
how this one fell. The only evidence
of his existence soon seeped
into the asphalt of another district.
At least there was that much.

I want too to be remembered,
but more blood will only dilute
those whose came before,
a diminishing return.

What I want to record most
is the simplicity of love I see
floating about the streets,
people accidentally finding
it just in time, right there,
maybe before being erased too.

I am being pretentious.
They must know it's love
in their meandering ways
of flirting: the raunchy jokes,
condensation of summer heat
beading down the bottle neck,
apparition of desire left behind
in the figure of a lone woman
vomiting in a back alley after
closing time, neon flickering
pink and yellow on her skin.

Let me bite you a little, just tender
enough to leave a small bruise, easily
hidden, that goes away in time.

11/06/19 (2)

Or so the collective chant goes,
but no, ideas are not bulletproof,
they can be usefully forgotten.
What did you do a month ago?

Truth is, I want you to be safe,
want you to sleep so I can sleep.
It's why I can never be a parent,
loving a brat like you.

No, ideas are not bulletproof.
They don't break because
they are not true, they break
with age, with convenience.

It's not what you want to hear,
it's not what I want to tell,
but here we are, looking
into each other as tho
we don't recognize who
we were to each other.

It's not what you want to bear,
but here we are, here at last.

11/07/19

Your face, turning away,
suggests otherwise.
There is no shame in wanting
to be more beautiful,

whatever happiness it is
you find in your secrecy
behind your hair trellising
the meridian of your back.

What is it you wish for me
to witness? You are enough
in your own—too much, really.
My desire is a simple beast.

May I be beautiful in your hunger.
Sitting bedside, the news unfurling
on TV before we undress for sex
or sleep, the city burning beneath us.

Take off your clothes. Let me find
who you've been holding in
behind, fuck whatever else
is burning. Let it all burn.

11/07/19 (2)

The graduation ceremony
had to end early, the chancellor
left with guards. Students
held signs in black gowns, saying,
"You can't kill us all."
How do we live up to that?

Inaudible, the sound of choice
midst human traffic.

These are our flesh and blood
until they are not, then poof,
they leave our nests, wear masks,
business as usual.
                 This too is not
blood on our hands, these hands
not our hands, rinsed clean
by the blood of another's lamb.

11/07/19 (3)

I am trying to gather myself
for another night.

Gear: check,
who I'll become:
check.
       Just another face
in a sea of crowd who loves
with fists.
          They haven't tried
me yet,
       I am still good.

I have forgotten why I am
out here
       aside from protecting
those whom I can call
          brother, sister;
they will never know my name.

Sometimes, the body impels,
and I follow,
       watching myself
as tho through a film,
          amid
the noise echoing
          in these tunnels.
The nation's anthem ends
with
    "forward, forward"
          and I am trying
to honour that,

            as faithful
as your native son,

                flowing unabided

    as water.

11/07/19 (4)

Don't call them dogs.
Protest is merely a sound
for ears that must stay deaf
for those who feed above.

They are more bothersome,
just as you are bothersome
as a roach, they are people
who have reasons of their own.

Reasons that put a baton
to the nape of your back, whisper
in your ear, "but breathe."

So breathe. Keep breathing
because death is not an option
unless you be among the meek.
Keep going, add fuel, a solution
will figure itself out.

Where you stand, winning
or not, at least you'll leave
a shoe print, your place in the sand
at the beach we grew up with,
popsicle juice dripping—remember
the romance you exist within.

11/07/19 (5)

The moon is out outright, despite
halved, despite behind the tear gas.
Chinese poets have written about it

tirelessly, across history, trying to
catch its meaning, to say "I'm here"
while things happen on the ground.

That is what I am looking at,
clouds slouching to obscure it,
bear with me for a moment longer:

There was a story we grew up with, of a master archer who shot down
nine suns, leaving only one to illuminate the world. Given immortal
elixir for what he managed, a prize generations of emperors spent
countless lives of their subjects on, our hero nevertheless either forgot
to drink it, or left it with his wife, Chang'e, as a gift, or for safekeeping.
On a mid-autumn day, while our hero departed for the day's hunt,
his friend tried to steal the potion and his wife, in a moment of panic,
drank it, became a goddess, living forever on the moon on her own,
longing for the archer who had long ago become history, become dust.

That is to say: I'm not a hero,
you are not a goddess,
neither of us will live forever.

This moon will keep hanging in
the night, beyond the future
stories others will invent.

That is not to say we never existed,
a single story, among many
that happened in our small epoch.

11/08/19

This is how it may start to end,
round of applause for the chief exec
to exit, quaintly hugging
in a photo op her family,
handshake, flowers.

There is no such easy exit tho,
one side wants blood,
the other penance,
and she must feign a decision
between staying and going.

I've never given so much thought
to anyone who stands before
a podium, prim and proper.
What may not be apparent
is that we too have given all we can,
so what's left? Choices
that cannot be choices
she presents.
                    Behind the lectern
then, she nods at the city's voices
and mustn't hear, because that
is her function, duty, to keep us safe,
harbour us from our own darkness.
Maintaining a steely certainty,
she looks into the camera, makes mention
of "law and order," "regretful that..."

Joss paper tossed in the air,
cinching as tho a salient joke,
asking "what if, what if."

11/08/19 (2)

Steadily the children queue up one by one
to be the latest face of martyrdom;
they deem it an illegal assembly.

A few faces are unpixelated at last
once the tabloids sell out, had the vessels
left thru unluckier doors.

Some mourners are afraid to go out,
some mourners take to the streets
while they still have a breath to hide,
unsure if the salt is their own or
cajoled by the harbour's new fragrance.

Please stop dying. we can't kill
you all, cells are running out
save prison up-border—
origami cranes we string together
as hope are paper coffins.

Now I know why the security
camera must look away,
it's not made to break our heir's fall.

11/08/19 (3)

They can be quiet too,
pay respects to one of their own
when tonight I thought the city
would be painted red. News
channels turn away, don't know
how to live-report the youthful hush.

One of the most terrifying sayings
in my mother tongue, no parents
ever want to utter,
"white hair giving away the black,"
while these kids have the dignity
to give away their black to their black.

Would be too easy to frame it
as attending their own funeral,
no, they are breaking through doors
we never had the courage even
to leave ajar. In their solemn
pause for silence, we respond with,
"be silenter."
                They are not listening,
too busy arranging candle pots
into a slogan of their time.

11/09/19

You holding my head down,
not letting me up for air,
clutching onto my hair until
you can petite-mort
                        so I kneel,
pry your legs apart in the shower,
searching for the tenderest
part of you with eyes closed,
to keep water from getting in.

Behind my eyes I am dreaming
another you, whom I knew
when we were young,
whom later I love.
When we step out, our heap
collapses into bed, you clutch
into me, weeping.
                        It's okay,
my bully. This is sometimes
how we must hold on
together, to hold, be held,
if it tires us into sleep
by one another,
                        for another night.

I love the way you snore,
my big baby, love your warmth
curved around my body. Inside you
I dream too if I am still there, my arm
clasped around you like a harness.

11/09/19 (2)

Detected in the scent of blood willing
ears perked up high, preachers scutter
from the cracks to gift white knuckles
our white benediction. None of you
had the gift to be the next Savonarola.

Waving a bible in your hand is not
the same as a pulpit. The good book
can't be simplified like that, it's not law
nor can late scripture carry weight.
Mark our dates:

6:9, we walked together
when we were still innocent.

6:12, a city of flameless smoke.

7:1, the Walls of Jericho fell.

7:21, when people in white tees
broke the rules of engagement.

8:31, dreamt ghosts wisp thru the subway gates.

11:8, a body certified dead,
we prayed him into some heaven.

In your next sermon, have the grace
to mark the graves of our siblings,   .
who grew brave, didn't ask
to become angels, did not insist
on wings. We can read just fine.

11/11/19

Necessity is the mother of invention
but the city is running out of material.
Tho the young keep impressing,
behind a secret of umbrellas
the frontline dreams a catapult
from scaffold of bamboo stalks.

A friend, when in Romania, gushed on
about pep rallies students held
to sever blood debt, same two words
scrawled across the walls here,
minus the romance among
the Montagues & Capulets.

The pen, in cahoots with the sword,
marks where the angels fear to tread,
the heiress of a foodservice giant
came to know after pronouncing,
"The city can survive without two
generations," her inheritance smashed
to bits daily by those who refuse
to honour her prognosis.

When the gas canisters are exhausted
by night, neighbours perch before sleep
by their flats' peeked curtains, caw
"Add fuel!"
                    Their neighbours parrot the same,
cooing for an instant into the sudden
morning like gossiping lovebirds, knowing
midst their aviary there are ears.

11/11/19 (2)

On one screen of a darkened mall,
paramedics chase for a real
or fictive ghost, reporters trailing
close behind for the same
tangled fibre of her white dress.

Two black-clad men lean
over the railing, gauging
the scene a storey above.

Red and blue lights refract
off the mall's glass exterior,
marching towards their own
conclusions, charging ahead
for whoever may be waiting
worthy of their rescue.

On the second screen, in another
district, silhouette of a figure
stands before a bonfire, blocking
the firemen from extinguishing.
Another screen, a fireman
beefs with the police.
And who have I become, behind
this screen, watching the reporters?

11/12/19

Police return to universities
to visit their younger siblings
who have taken up a course
in archery. During today's press
conference yesterday's stats:
287 arrested, 209 male, 81 female,
aged 12-82. Do the math.

A reporter among reporters asks
why an officer ventriloquised
a limp student as tho still conscious.
An officer PRs a ventriloquised reply.

No longer will tired bodies fall
parallel along the city's vertical,
but random objects onto coming
traffic, tho there's little traffic
left to aim for. Repurposed items
litter the streets, made useful again
by their inconvenience, awaiting
a katamari ball to pick them up.

How long can a metro pause
before it becomes a ruin?
The opposing answers yawn
across the aisle towards the same
concluding "fuck your mom!" yawp
on the campus ground.

THIS AREA
KEEP OUT
WEAR RESPIRATORY PRO

警告
前方曾被施放中國制催淚彈
此地帶已被二噁英污染

THIS AREA HAS BEEN CONTAMINATED
WITH DIOXIN

KEEP OUT
WEAR RESPIRATORY PROTECTION

警告
前方曾被施放中國制催淚彈
此地帶已被

THIS AREA HAS B
WITH

11/12/19 (2)

The sumptuous life we've been
dreaming was never feasible
but one we all idle about, possibilities
of what we'd do if we won the lotto.

How we'd take our friends away
on trips, fat meals for our family,
a modest ring for a beloved,
how we would take them out
of rooms into small apartments.

The horse track has no horses
out, their musculature nothing
left to analyze.
                        A councillor
stutters, offers up advice to supplant
what he is too incompetent to fix. So
police must become his shield
and billy club against the onslaught
of his own failing.
                        A peace offering
from the sage to us children:
"you only have one life to live,"
as tho yolo needs to don a hard hat.

The horses can never be released
into the wild, we know, no one
has asked for those green hills.
All that we want is the chance
to hold our umbrellas upward again,
for all the fire and smoke
we began to dissipate, give us rain,
rain to bead on a spider's silk.

11/13/19

I told you women are tougher
than men, did you not see the fear
in her eyes when the po po carted her
off in the cruiser? Gang rape allegedly, ˙

Siu mai, ten for a skewer, eighteen two.

but we've heard all the details
for the inquest underway to matter.
They too are looking for the father
of the student's, in the tissue sample
of the aborted fetus with a warrant.
Who knows,

Here, two dollars change.

         it could be her boyfriend's.

Too bad it's not like American TV,
the spectacle of a contestant running
victory laps for an offspring not their own,
but this show here is as close as it gets.

Bowl of beef offal? Thirty.

The girl in the van tho, I worry
she's too cute for her own good.

11/14/19

Politics play out on playgrounds
too, boarding schools arrange
buses to escort kids from mainland
home.
      Innocence is a construct,
as is power, but the latter
more visceral, quicker to absorb
when all it takes is four fingers
to learn how they can roll into
the palm, the thumb locking
a fist into place.
      Now they can ape
a reason at the monkey bars,
looking up to their black-clad siblings,
a reason as easily found as a knife
one kitchen shelf too high.

How much do you suppose
your little brother loves you, wants
to protect you from a bogeyman?

11/16/19

I used to be a teacher.
What am I to say
when a student responds,
after confessing I am
too chicken shit to stay,
"We'll fight for all of us"?

They announce their names,
yelling "I will not kill myself"
while being dragged away,
in case their name is mistaken
for one fallen by mistake.

The student is still
messaging me via
an encrypted app, assuring
he's safe for my sake.

If you were to die,
don't die for my sake.
Die of old age, one
neither of us can envision;
die for love, die of earned
sadness, sickness, but
not for this, not now,
wait it out til
my parents die,
til I die, stay.

11/17/19

Sorry I haven't written lately,
winter is fast approaching, etc.
Neither the emperor
or the students have any clothes.

Fortified behind their respective walls
of legislature and campus,
the police in between are prying
at a resolution, trying to storm
a burning bridge while students stand
pat or slip into sewer grates.
Beside it one of the city's arterial
tunnels connects the island
to the mainland, suspended, day 3.

Molotovs blossom everywhere.
Overseas diners debate behind
a glass pane, staff jamming
wet towels under the front door,
about the merit of a reporter
who ran past, disappeared into smoke.

The PLA made a guest appearance
yesterday, parading down
a local street to clear it of its bricks.

I've been scribbling for poems,
plucked off the streets last night
a used gas canister I use as paper
weight for luck, size of a cicada's shell.
What's left inside don't smell so bad
but I won't tempt the gods, mami.

11/21/19

It's as tho we were separated
at birth, our backs touching
because we weren't taught
how to ask for love. I want to turn
towards you, ask about your day
but we both know the answer.
We made it out, what else
is there to say? Come inside me,
you ask before our contiguity.
No borders worth uncrossing
anymore if there's no tomorrow
tho that's not the destination
I want, I want to move slowly
as possible, to be connected
to you, melt back into you
for as long as I can, curling
our bodies into two question marks.
But you know biology must take
over eventually, it is the destiny
of men. Love me then, you ask,
thru the only way I can love you
in this minute of desperation,
let's find a way out thru our skin
as if there can be a way out.

11/22/19

Feel that spot, the soft cartilage
at the bottom of the sternum
where the rib cage splits?
Just below that is where
the diaphragm is. Ow, yes, there.

Aim there. Knuckle of your index finger
jutted—I love your delicate fingers;
they won't be able to breathe
for a few seconds, run then.

If they come at you with an extendo,
just above the elbow, if you can
grab hold, apply pressure
behind the tendons, they must
drop what's in their hand.

If you are surrounded, lie down
in fetal position, pretend to be
a kid again, do not resist.
If you are surrounded later, pretend
to be a woman, shit yourself, do not
give them the pleasure.
Stay quiet. Remember my name.

In the father's eulogy to Tsz-Lok Chow,
or Alex, "My Child, your responsibility
is complete. I am proud of you."
The second clause could translate
as "Your mission is complete,"
"You have met my expectations,"
or "Your duty has ended."
What he refused to utter
are the three simple words.

It is an ironic and ambiguous language,
my mother tongue. How then do I tell
you I love you, which inflection
would carry the weight of what I mean?
If only it was as simple as the street food
vendor I frequent who said "20 dollars,"
before I had a chance to order,
us grinning at each other,
a moment of connection
in this despairing city.   So tell me,
across our divide, I love you, say it,
accidental as a tuning fork dropped
onto the floor, resounding within me.

11/26/19

The city is singing Hallelujah to the lord,
a city the lord had suddenly refound—
to whom do you keel gracefully for?

We all know how this is going to end.
In the sudden quiet, we scurry to see
family again, be lovely to each other.

It isn't an anthem of protest you hear,
it is a recalling, echoing through what
we want to remember as our home.

No, destroy it. What will be gone is already gone.
Remake our world, let's see how you manage.

11/26/19 (2)

The Christmas tree in the mall is ablaze.
Maybe we aren't spirits seeing this, maybe
we're telegraphing what we want done.

Nor was it ever a tree, by the smell
of its burning— something plastic,
something poetic. The lights draped over
a commercial high-rise, in the shape
of a dove, inviting Christmas, insist.

Let's Christmas then. I am so tired of all this.
I know you are too. Remember when
we cha-chaed? Sculpture of our legs,
fingers prodded into the other's waist.
Organized violence is just that, didn't happen
out of the blue.
                    Those who are blind to it,
take a number and wait to be called.
Lock-stepped, we hurdle towards our turn,
erotic for blood without ever asking,
a hand extended to catch, to be caught,
neither can play the hand of the saviour's.

11/27/19

Birds become lyrical at the sound
of the word, find poetry: death.
Tweet. We are not there yet,
hence our pointlessness in between.

Embroidered in love, in Klimt's painting
the face of the paramour turns away
as tho the one without power.
I am trying my damndest to reclaim
my language, to amp the volume
of your hair midst the mock chorus
in our city.
                    There is an eternal song
that has eluded Cat Power all these years
playing in the reverbing apartment.
Kiss or be kissed, what matters
is the now between sutured lips.
While the ferry ferries back and forth,
while people get to work, off work. Look up,
the birds have alit, they chirp for us.

11/27/19 (2)

Document the brief life I have
had with you. Note the contours
of my clavicles, times when I chortle
at your jokes, days when I retreat
into myself, trying to contain it.

No answers to avail, time better
spent with you, but I had to look,
to find someone worth your time,
we haven't got much left.

This is what I will remember:
your outtie belly button,
your rehearsed fury at the waiter
the time when the food ran late,
knives and forks suspended in the air.
The way you snickered beneath
the orange-lit alleyway, taking off
your respirator to win a dare, you twerp.

Before we grow up into others,
remember our pulsing hearts
pressed against each other's,
palm to palm. We were young.
Let's not forget our errors.

11/29/19

My sister orders my favourite snack,
deep-fried capelins, each fish within it
a genocide, we used to joke, 80%
of its weight made of roe.

                             "Eat,"
she humbles, pushes the plate
toward me. I haven't the stomach
for days. Had the government known
the ache in the years we hid
behind our backs, they wouldn't need
to build a new campus for detainees
across the border, the old one still
smoldering.
                    I take one in my mouth,
the oil on its ruptured skin glistens.

On the way home in these now-calmed streets,
leaning under the steady sign of a 7-11,
I am eating its ready-made sui loong bao,
or *Xiao Long Bao*. They mean the same thing,
little dragon bun. Tho I fear I am unsure
when time will come to know which
enunciation will be the correct one.

11/29/19 (2)

"I don't want your business," the funeral director said plainly to a pair of customers whose child fell off the balcony for undisclosed reasons.

They don't need you, there are other mortuaries in wait.

I can't keep writing about this, my fury is beside the point. How his parents must have felt crackling under their skin, trying to make way for a private grief.

"Renovation" made its way into common parlance here.

Burn, ashes to ashes; the unlit body, an unlit house.

12/01/19

First rubber, then lead-copper polymer,
now back to teak. Siphoned thru taps
in Cambodia, transacted thru Thailand;
mined in China, Chile; who knows
where the wood comes from.
The body is 60% water, we are barely
made of flesh to sustain the harder materials.
In a rare off-night when I could dream,
I was back in the classroom, blindly
teaching "Methoughts I Saw my Late
Espoused Saint" to ears foreign
to its sound, too young to know the longing
it cleaved towards. The heat of my body,
distributed by the estuaries of my blood
made into existence by the blood
of my mother, my father, I became a body,
my body. What more can it have given
to the extinction of the next cohort,
should they deny their liability to shatter?

12/03/19

Looking down the barrel,
the shot misses, clinking
off the lip of the horn.
The cue ball fizzles away
from where I had planned
it off rail. She admires
the ambition nevertheless,
the thinness of the cut.

Stroke after stroke, she can't
make me come in the pool
hall bathroom. She isn't you,
she hasn't the knowledge
of how my body works,
the deftness of your hand
curling a loose lock of my wig
behind my ear, your face fading.

A street preacher gallivants
with a bullhorn towards me, rhymes,
"The officer has to stay at work late,
his wife has to stay home and masturbate."
I wouldn't have missed had I chosen
to raise my gun, take aim, pop.

12/11/19

I'm not taking for granted
what you've built for me, dad,
a sentiment I can't tell you
across the lazy susan between
you and the uncles and aunties
stoking each other's belly fire.

That's still my dream, auntie,
going to fashion school, maybe
industrial design, I am learning
hands-on, bet you dunno what
the ridgeline on a hard hat's for.

Uncle, I know you love me and
you wouldn't think she deserved it
if you knew I was among them
come night when I must slip out
of my school uniform.

What you've afforded me, a good life,
bought you instead a conscience
that I insulate from you, knowing you
must insist it as teenage rebellion,
a phase. You went thru yours
at my age, after all. Tho the world
you grew out of and into is not
the one awaiting me, one even worse
for your grandkids if I don't preserve
what's left of your world to relay
into their hands.

This is why I go out after dinner,
why you stare into the TV
without a question or goodbye
as the hinges of the front door squeak
shut. I would much rather rest
my head on your lap, watch TV
and laugh with you at dumb rom-coms,
than psyching myself into courage
in the descending elevator.

Maybe when I'm back for good
we can take a family trip to Japan.
If I don't return, then you'll probably
be reading this right now.

In case I'm missing, let my say again
the obvious in the silence of my room:
You have done nothing wrong,
couldn't have been a better father,
sorry I was an ungrateful daughter.

But for now, here, let me pour you
more tea, divine in the leaves my love.

12/16/19

Fubar, this protest shit. It's simple
to forget that our muscles work
as a system of pulleys til a bone breaks
or tendon snaps, tension between
the same flesh slings far flung forward
then recoils in opposing direction
like frames of a foreign art film,
two lovers in a sepiatone train station
running towards the other, then past.

Snip the red strings between our hearts.
Snip our snow globe unus mundus,
or in my supposed inherent mother tongue,
yin/yang. Snip the corollary, coronary
sinew that once bound us together.

Snip then, the woman in the red dress
towing behind her a wheeled suitcase,
striding calmly from the maenads
haranguing after her, those who enact
who they are by who they are not.

Midst the motion of bodies, paused
in the background a granny stations
in her booth, her digital keyboard jangles
Rudolph the Red-Nosed Reindeer,
or in Gilbert's words, *refusing heaven.*

12/18/19

From the center of this byzantine map
I'm chasing after a kid who knows
every deke and alleyway that shapeshifts
away from me. I remember his thrill
acrobating thru the imaginary gauntlet
gargoyled by huddled haunches,
lithing his own thru pendulum axe elbows,
bodies blurring into the ghost cartography.

The strength and surety behind the start
of each wolf hair stroke, gliding
rough-hewn as far as the ink needs
to travel, then settles, eventually,
fanning into the edgeless tabula rasa
of a nameless future, black sheen
drying dull on sandalwood paper.

Whoso list to hunt then, Mini-Me,
together we disappear ceaselessly.

Fingers crossed as others' have too
within their nebulous pinpoints
worth preserving, arms of our gyres
catching each others', interlocking
our stories into tapestry lest
they fray singly into amnesia.

Better a tattered cloth steamed hot
against our cheeks than nothing
at all about the mishmash fiction
of an existed town, recounted
thru binoculars from an elsewhere
terra firma, calligraphic script hanging
above ethereal mountains, before them
insinuation of greener pasture opening
behind us, beckoning us back up the hills—

to watch and wait for the last sun to rise
over us as apartment lights dim one by one,
wait, to be exhumed from our stony sleep.

07/01/20

07/02/20

The |

Notes

P. 13: Actual quotes from the three political figures listed.

P. 38: "Like water" is a resistance tactic adapted by protesters, rooted in Bruce Lee's philosophy (which is in turn informed by Taoist philosophy of the mythical Lao Tzu) behind his self-formulated *Jeet Kune Do* martial art style which emphasizes reactive nimbleness against its opponent's offense.

P. 39: "Cockroach" (甲由) is a derogatory term for protesters, who have since adopted it as a badge of honour.

P. 41: "Add fuel" (加油) is a literal translation of a popular idiom that gesticulates encouragement.

P. 43: Hong Kong translates literally as "Fragrant Harbour."

P. 48: Actual quote from Annie Wu Suk-ching (伍淑清), the daughter of the founder of the Maxim Group, one of the largest conglomerate foodservice providers in Hong Kong.

P. 50: "Katamari" is a popular Japanese video game series where a "prince" character rolls a sticky ball across various terrain to pick up strewn-about objects with the goal of amassing as much weight as possible within a time limit.

P. 51: Dioxin is the chief carcinogen in tear gas most concerning from a public health perspective.

P. 52: Actual quote from a pro-government district councilor.

P. 57: "Blossom everywhere" (遍地開花) is a not-so-secretive codename for a then-newly implemented tactic by protesters where riots break out spontaneously in as many districts as possible to stretch police resources and their ability to focus on any one specific riot site.

P. 67: "Renovation" (裝修) is an euphemism used by rioters to connote vandalism.

P. 70: "The officer has to stay at work late, / his wife has to stay home and masturbate" was an overheard rhyming couplet in Cantonese (the primary Chinese dialect spoken in Hong Kong, as opposed to Mandarin which is commonly used in most of mainland China) during a protest march, uttered to taunt riot police on standby.

P. 73: Someone dragging a suitcase behind them in Hong Kong is usually a signal of a visiting mainland tourist, purchasing goods at a discount and/or of a better quality.

Notable Dates

6/9/19: The first large scale protest march in 2019. CHRF estimated that 1.03 million people participated to protest the upcoming second reading of the extradition amendment bill that would legalize the extradition of fugitives sought by countries with whom Hong Kong has no extradition agreements with, namely, China, whose opaque judicial system Hong Kongers find suspect. They also fear trumped up charges for financial or political reasons.

6/12/19: Approximately 40,000 protesters gathered around the Legislative Council Building to disrupt, successfully, the second reading of the extradition amendment bill. Violence between police and protesters escalated, most notably the usage of rubber bullets and beanbag rounds as crowd control tools that have not been seen in action for decades on Hong Kong soil.

Various organized strikes, sit-ins, and store closures paralyzed the city. The following day, for the first time police used the term "rioters" during a press conference. Carrie Lam announced the suspension of the bill two days after that.

6/16/19: The largest protest march to date, estimated to be a hair shy of 2 million by CHRF. The primary objective was to request a complete withdrawal, rather than a moratorium, of the extradition bill.

The march also mourned the first official fatality related to the extradition bill; 35 year-old protester Marco Leung Ling-Ki (梁凌杰) who fell to his death by accident from the roof of a shopping mall while unfurling an anti-extradition bill banner a day before.

Lastly, the march also helped finalize the articulation of the four core demands announced publicly two days after (the fifth, the resignation of Carrie Lam and universal suffrage of legislative council and chief executive elections, was formalized later), which are:

1. Complete withdrawal of the extradition bill
2. The discontinuation of mislabeling of protests as riots, the latter of which carries with it possibility of criminal prosecution
3. Release and exoneration of arrested protesters
4. The creation of an independent commission of inquiry that has legal teeth to investigate and prosecute police misconduct

7/1/19: On the 22nd anniversary of Hong Kong's handover back to China, CHRF organized a protest march in the afternoon, estimated to have been attended by a quarter-million people. Later in the evening, a splinter group of rioters stormed the Legislative Council Building and vandalized the interior. Eight days later, Carrie Lam announced that the extradition bill was officially "dead."

7/21/19: 100+ mob sporting white shirts and metal rods rushed into Yuen Long subway station to indiscriminately attack protesters, commuters, civilians, media staff and pro-democratic lawmaker Lam Cheuk-Ting (林卓廷), inside the station and subway cars. Some believe or are suspicious of collusion between the police and local rural village members due to the tardiness of police arrival at the scene, eye witness accounts of police officers and white-shirts conversing at and leaving the scene together after the attack, and that some of the white-shirts have criminal records related to triad activities.

A documentary producer, Choy Yuk-Ling (蔡玉玲), who investigated the Yuen Long attack and possible police misconduct, was arrested shortly after the TV program was aired, charged with falsifying information for submitting an erroneous request for security footage to the Transportation Department that captured the license plates of two get-away vehicles registered under local village leaders in Yuen Long.

8/11-12/19: A two-day tactical protest was executed at the Hong Kong International Airport to garner more international attention and disrupt flight traffic, causing hundreds of canceled flights and many more delays. A female medic was shot in the eye by a pellet round at another protest site in Tsim Sha Tsui, leading to a retributive mood on the 12th. Two suspected PRC reporters were beaten at the airport by splinter rioters, while healthcare professionals held rallies at hospitals to denounce police violence against the medic.

8/31/19: Described sarcastically as the "police version of 7/21," violence broke out after a protest within Prince Edward subway station, as described by South Morning China Post (SCMP)[1]:

> "Unprecedented scenes of violence played out in Hong Kong's MTR network on the night of Saturday, August 31, as police stormed into Prince Edward station and beat protesters on a train.
> Protesters and their supporters accused police of beating commuters indiscriminately, but police said they were going after radicals who had changed their clothes and were pretending to be passengers.

---

1   SCMP; Sept 2, 2019: https://www.scmp.com/video/hong-kong/3025404/more-60-people-arrested-violence-erupts-hong-kongs-prince-edward-mtr

(Credit: anon, LIHKG, CC by 2.0)

Members of the police Special Tactical Squad, known as the Raptors[2], entered the station after the MTR reported that protesters were vandalising the premises and fighting with passengers.

Sixty three people were arrested following violence in Prince Edward and Mong Kok stations, which remained closed on Sunday."

Allegations of civilian deaths surfaced shortly after MTR Corp's reluctance to provide video footage of the incident. Monthly protests and vigils have been held on every 31st of subsequent months. They have been met with arrests and ticketing for reasons ranging from illegal assembly, violation of COVID public gathering ordinance and littering of funereal bouquets and written letters left for the rumoured dead.

On April 15, 2021, Hong Kong celebrated its first "National Security Education Day," which, among other spectacles of patriotic education, included a simulation of the event for primary school children to reenact, the juxtaposition of images Hong Kong Police Chief Chris Tang cited as "misinformation" and promised future criminal investigation.

11/08/19: The date of death of Alex Tsz-Lok Chow (周梓樂), a 22 year old student protester, who suffered severe head injuries four days prior, after falling from the 3rd floor of a parking lot where nearby confrontations between protesters and the police were occuring. Circumstances leading to his fall are inconclusive; Chow's death served as the prelude to one of the most violent standoffs between protesters and the police up to that point in time and at the time of this writing.

11/11/19: Violence on both sides reached fever pitch. Vigilantism by radical splinter sect who referred to themselves as "Valiants"

---

2   Known in Cantonese idiom as "速龍小隊"

(勇武派) set a pro-government civilian on fire, following an earlier incident when the police shot a Valiant for the first time with live ammunition.

11/17/19-11/29/19: Arguably the most dramatic and violent protest incident of 2019, the siege of Hong Kong Polytechnic University (PolyU) began with protesters disrupting traffic by vandalizing toll booths and tossing debris from a footbridge connecting the Hung Hom Harbour to PolyU. The bridge is suspended over the Hung Hom entrance of the Cross-Harbour Tunnel connecting Hong Kong Island to the rest of Hong Kong.

Copying tactics employed a week earlier by protesters at Chinese University of Hong Kong (CUHK) where protesters fortified the campus as a stronghold and disrupted traffic nearby, the PolyU protesters met a much more coordinated and better equipped police battalion compared to the relatively peaceful disbandment of its CUHK predecessor. Police deployed their entire arsenal and in response the protesters raided the university's athletics equipment storage and chemistry lab to concoct more robust countermeasures. The protesters ultimately lost in the battle of attrition, with stragglers trying to escape in the late stages of the siege via ziplining, sewage tunnels, and rappelling from the footbridge to motorcycles waiting below. All in all, more than 1,100 people were arrested and 280 plus people injured in the nearly two-week standoff.

06/30/20: Within a single day, the government completed the passing, signing and commencement of the Nation Security Law (國家安全法), that "criminalizes subversion, secession, foreign interference and terrorist acts, which were broadly defined to include disruption to public transport and other infrastructure,"[3] with a potential sentence of life imprisonment.

---

3   The quoted summary of the National Security Law is taken from Hong Kong Free Press (https://hongkongfp.com/), an anglophone Hong Kong-based non-profit news organization.

The full text of the law came into light (or morning light, rather) and effect to the general public, including Carrie Lam[4], just before midnight of July 1st, coinciding with the founding day of the Chinese Communist Party.

The amendments as drafted are applicable to anyone within or without Hong Kong soil (e.g. those who have layovers at Hong Kong's airport). Theoretically, anyone on earth who has committed offences as dictated by the law can be charged and have a warrant issued for their arrest. Many western democratic countries have since nixed extradition agreements with China since the passage of the amendments. Crimes committed against China's National Security Law in countries where extradition agreements with China are still in place would fall under the jurisdiction of the host country to decide whether extradition would be warranted on a case-by-case basis.

Some legal experts in Hong Kong have communicated their reservations about the vagueness of the language in the law, as it may lend itself to selective enforcement and flexibility of interpretation, while some scholars in social sciences, intellectuals, and the general public have commented on the chilling effect the law has had on freedom of expression, the press, and assembly (including the indirect effect on internalized self-censorship; prior to the enactment of the law, many Hong Kong citizens began scrubbing their social media clean of any social and/or political content); lack of accountability regarding the increase of police jurisdiction and brutality; erosion of Common Law; dereliction of responsibility and duty of elected officials in their representation of their constituencies; fear of government surveillance, etc., all of which have been melded together under the umbrella term "White Terror" (白色恐怖).

---

4   BBC, June 30, 2019: https://www.bbc.com/news/world-asia-china-52765838

89

Acknowledgments

I would like to thank Albert Moritz, Maggie Clark, Ben Nolan, Tanya Decarie, Tom Bourguignon, Mercer Bufter, Heather Barnabe, Jacob Rakovan, Jenna Smith and David De Leon for giving this manuscript your attention while in its infancy and offering comments to help me shape it into what it has become now. An especial thank you to Richard Greene for your eternal encouragement and close eye to the poems as they came step by step into being.

To my editor Jim Johnstone, thank you for being a worthy challenger while we butted heads in the manuscript's honing, in your cultural knowledge and sensitivity to know when to step in and when to leave things be so that I had the necessary space to operate in my janky patois and imagination without sounding like a lunatic.

To my publisher Aimee Parent Dunn, thank you for welcoming me into the Palimpsest family and taking the manuscript under its roof on such short notice. Had I tried for a Hong Kong press, this little sliver of a love song would likely have been censored out of existence.

Thank you to Chris Gaul for allowing me to use the fantastic and on-point photo from your "Hong Kong Erasure" series (readers: please check out the rest of the series and his other projects at chrisgaul.net), I am so heartened to see someone with your keen eyes see the same thing I thought I saw. Thank you also to Ellie Hastings for translating the image into the book cover faithfully.

I am grateful to the editors of *Voice & Verse Poetry Magazine, Half a Grapefruit, Juniper, Bosphorus Review of Books, Rice*

Paper, Eksentrika, Third Estate Art, Trinity Review, Qwerty, The Fiddlehead, The Bombay Review, Mekong Review, New Contrast, The /tɛmz/ Review, and the *Literary Review of Canada* for publishing some of the poems at various stages of maturity in this collection.

Lastly and most importantly, thank you Hongers, for reminding me of the clay I'm made of. For those of you who have chosen to stay or cannot leave, I admire so much your necessary bravery. For those who have joined the diaspora, we must do our part. 我哋真係好撚鍾意香港, let's never forget; wherever we may be, let's keep the sun from ever setting under our rialto.

#香港人加油 #StandWithHongKong #MilkTeaAlliance

Sam Cheuk is the author of *Love Figures* (Insomniac Press, 2011) and *Deus et Machina* (Baseline Press, 2017). He holds an MFA in creative writing from New York University and BA in English literature from University of Toronto. He is currently working on the second half of the diptych, tentatively titled *Marginalia*, which examines the function, execution, and generative potential behind censorship.